FREE AUDIOBOOK

In a land where the sun kisses the sky,
The Aztecs built their empire so high.
With their temples tall and a culture so grand,
Let's embark on a journey to this magical land.

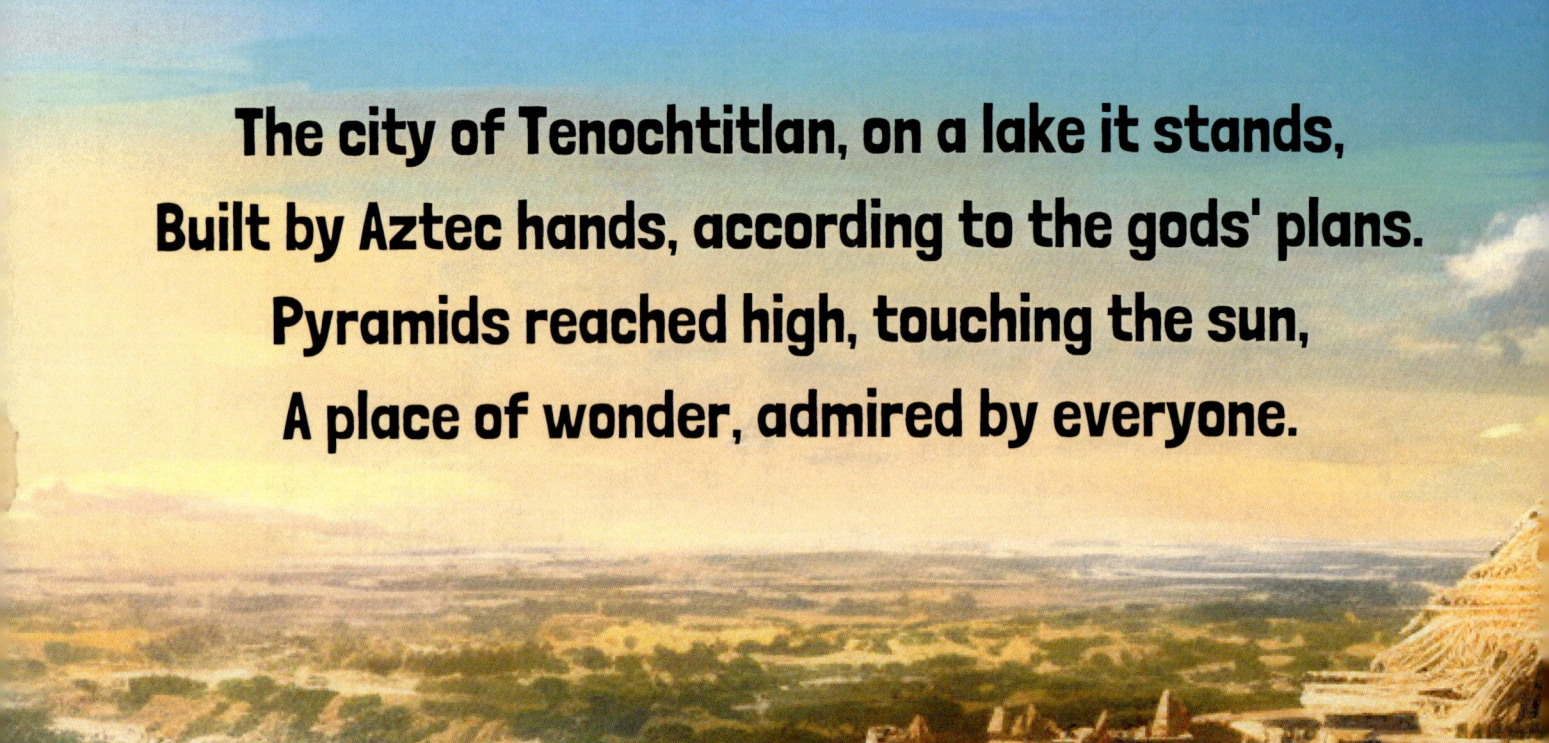

The city of Tenochtitlan, on a lake it stands,
Built by Aztec hands, according to the gods' plans.
Pyramids reached high, touching the sun,
A place of wonder, admired by everyone.

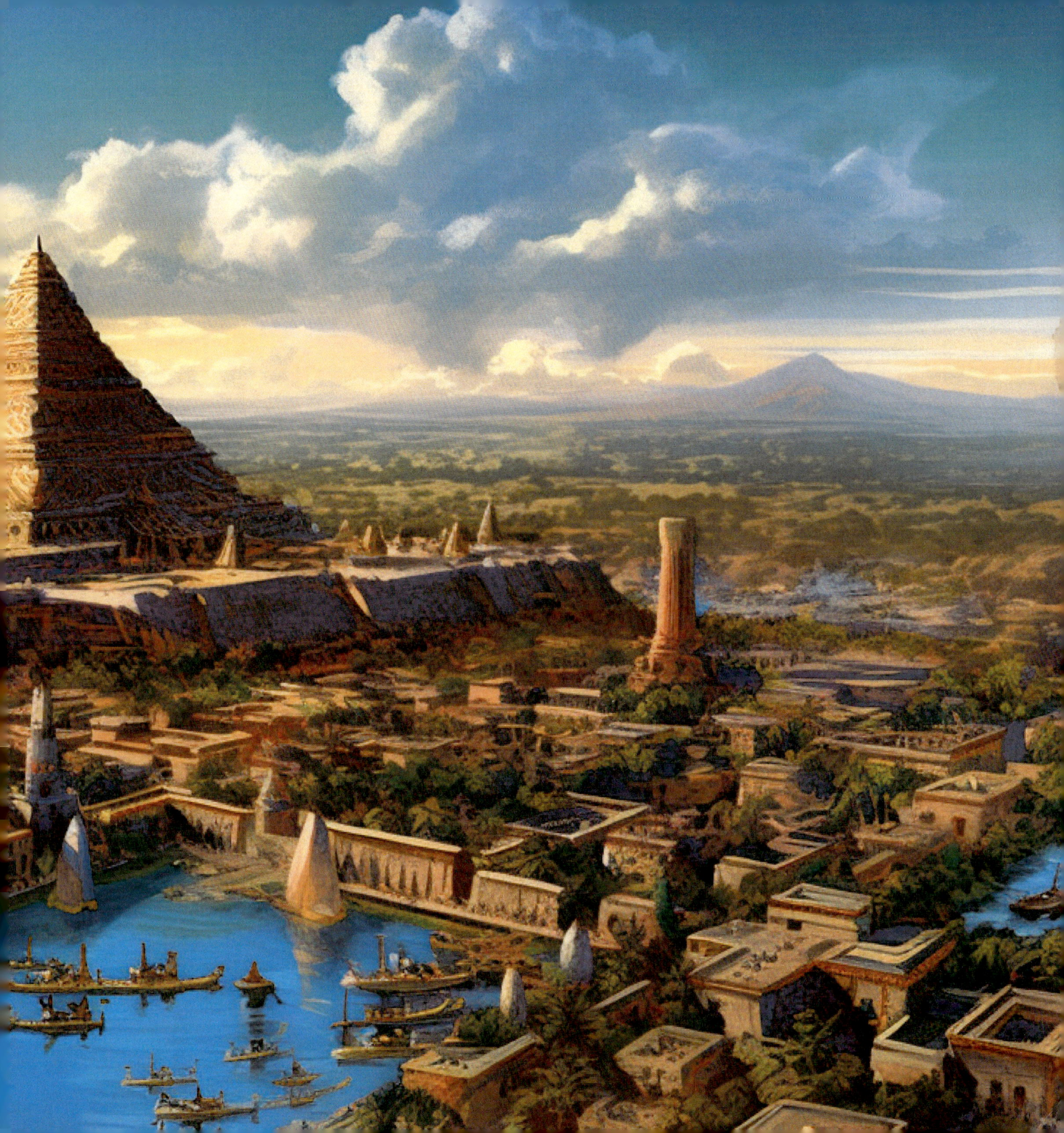

Aztec warriors, brave and bold,
Their tales of courage, often told.
Feathers and shields, in their hands held high,
Their fierce cries echoing in the sky.

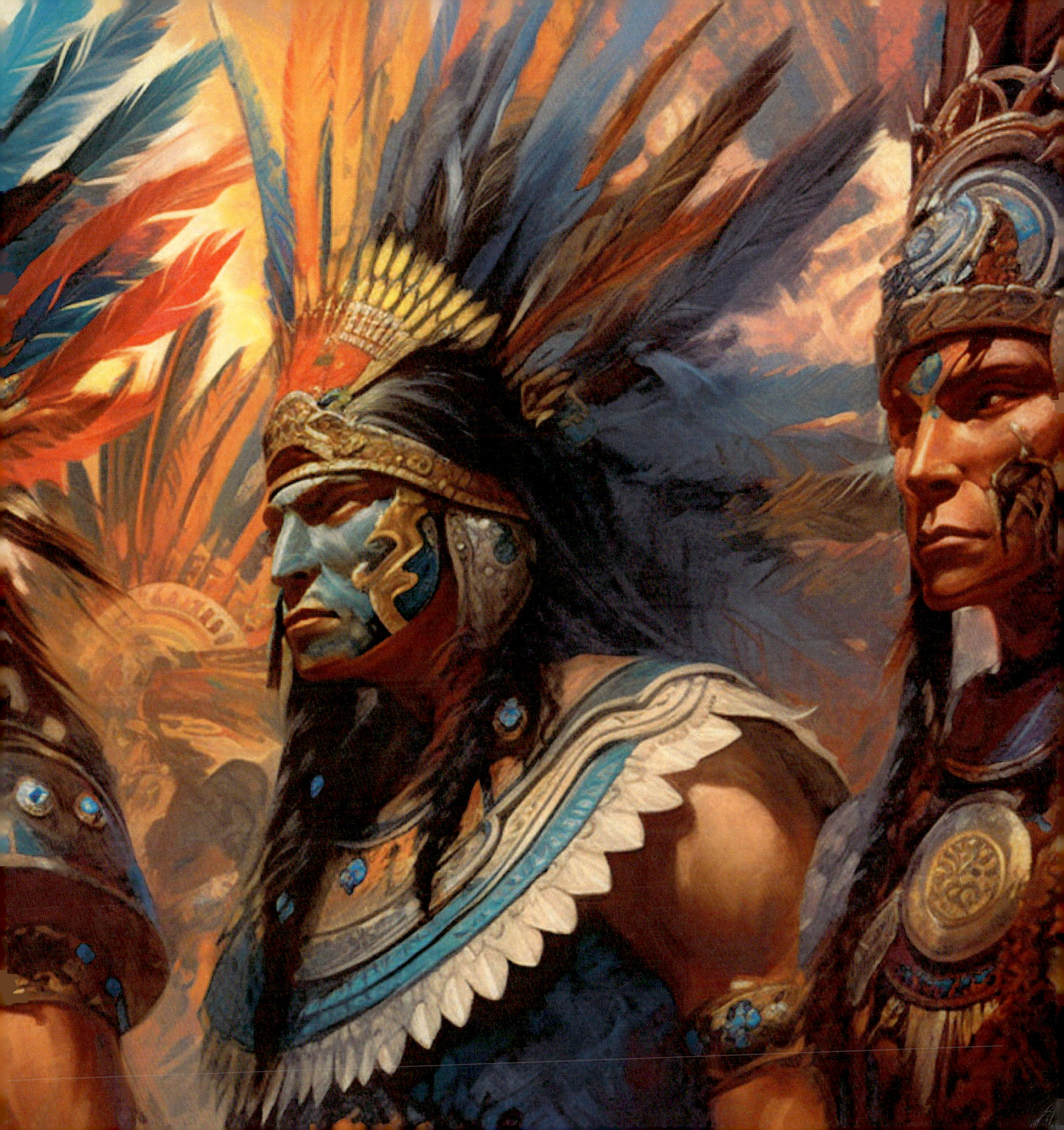

A calendar round, carved in stone,
Marking time in a rhythm of its own.
Three hundred sixty-five days it counts,
In the passing of time, every second amounts.

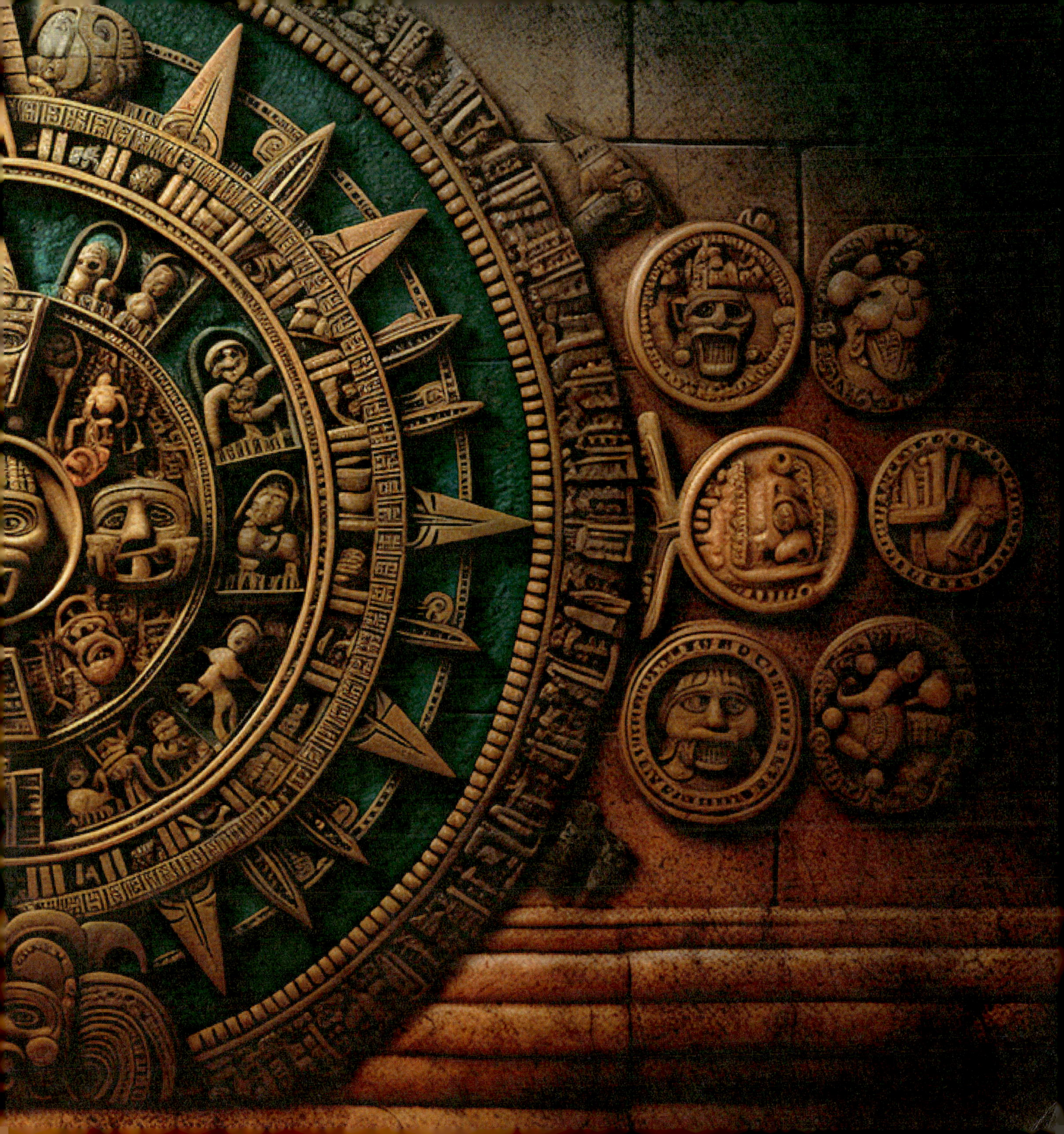

The Aztecs loved their games, oh so much,
The ball court's echoes, walls did touch.
A rubber ball, through stone rings thrown,
Victory's sweet taste, to the winners known.

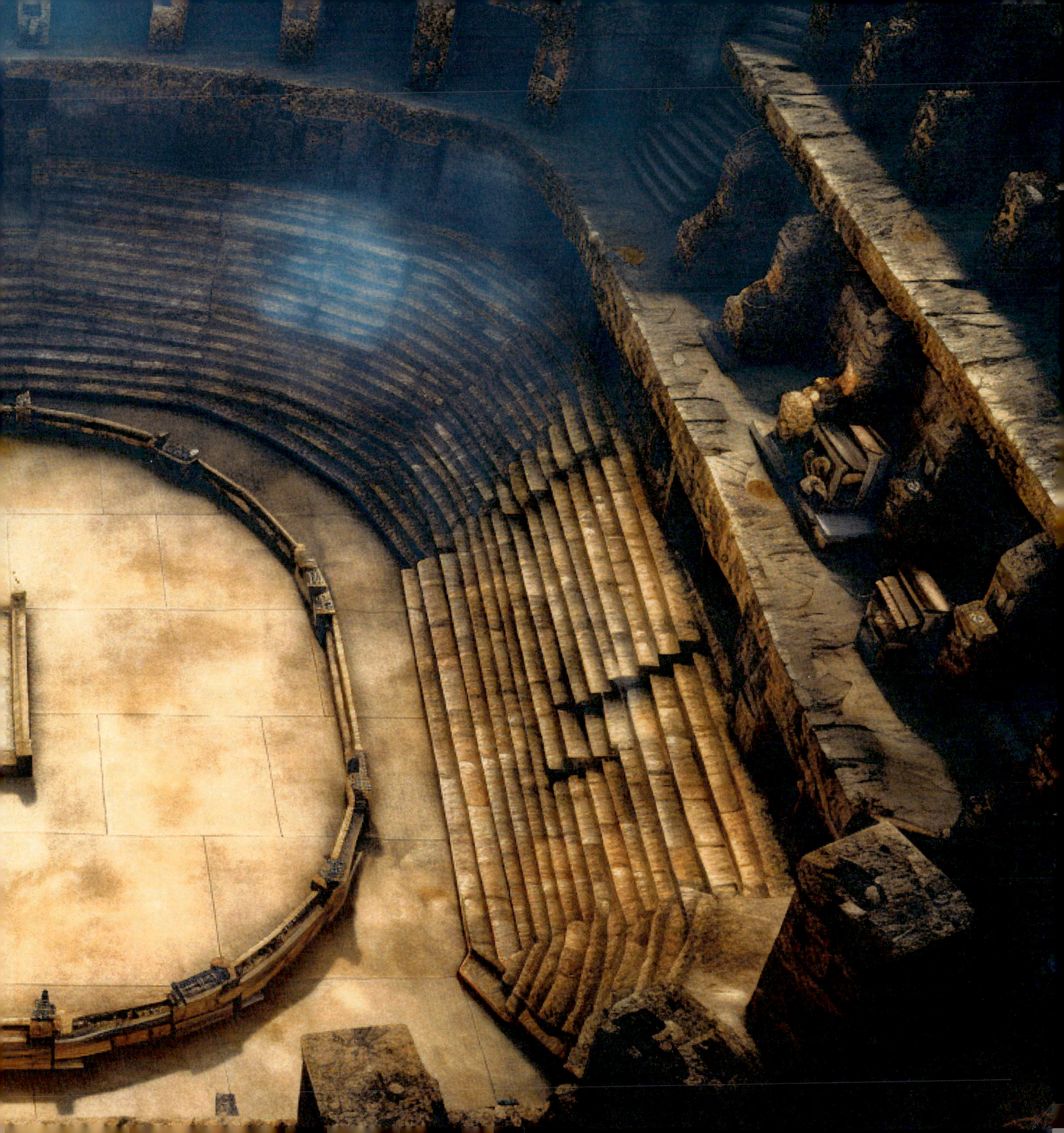

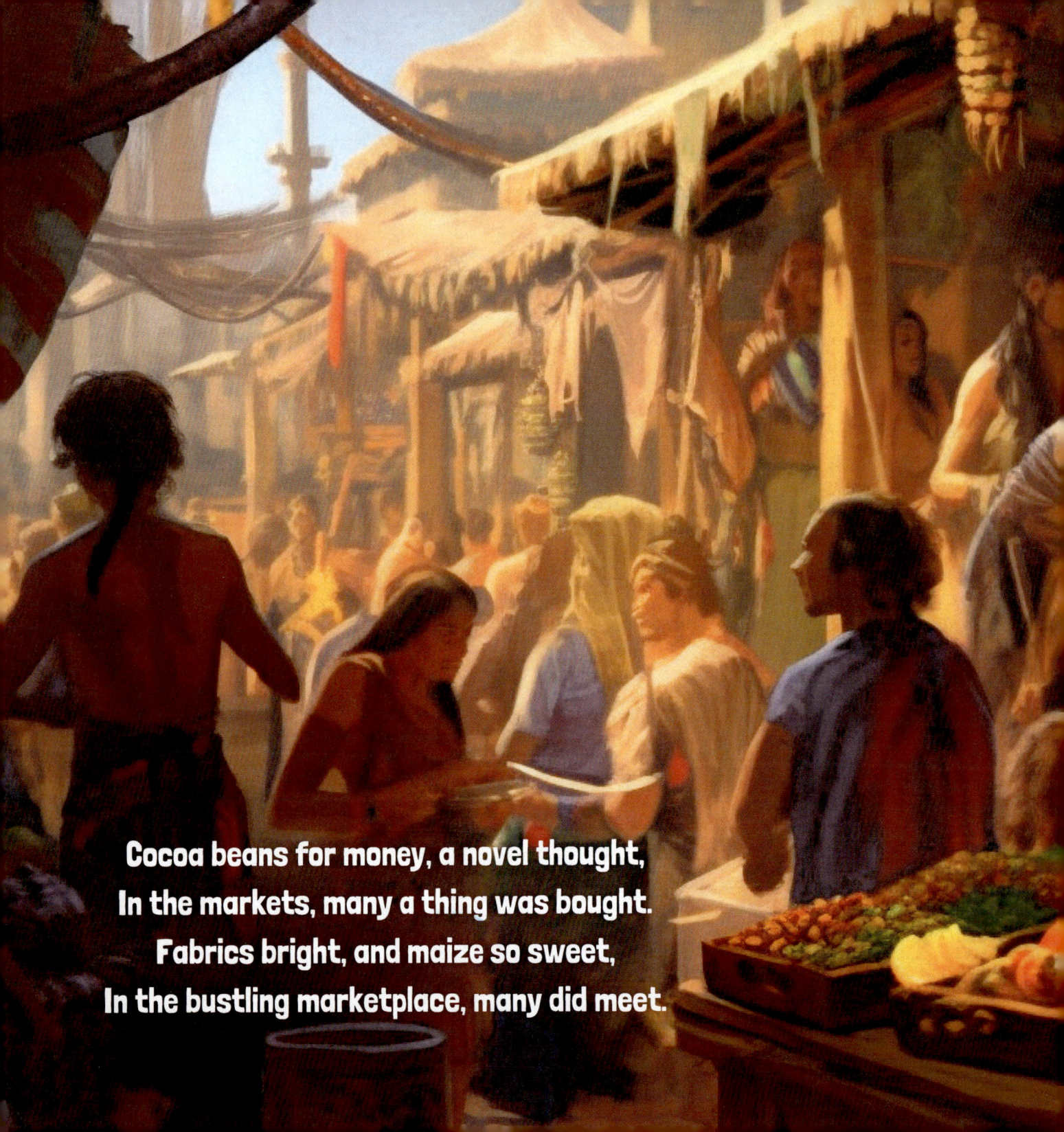

Cocoa beans for money, a novel thought,
In the markets, many a thing was bought.
Fabrics bright, and maize so sweet,
In the bustling marketplace, many did meet.

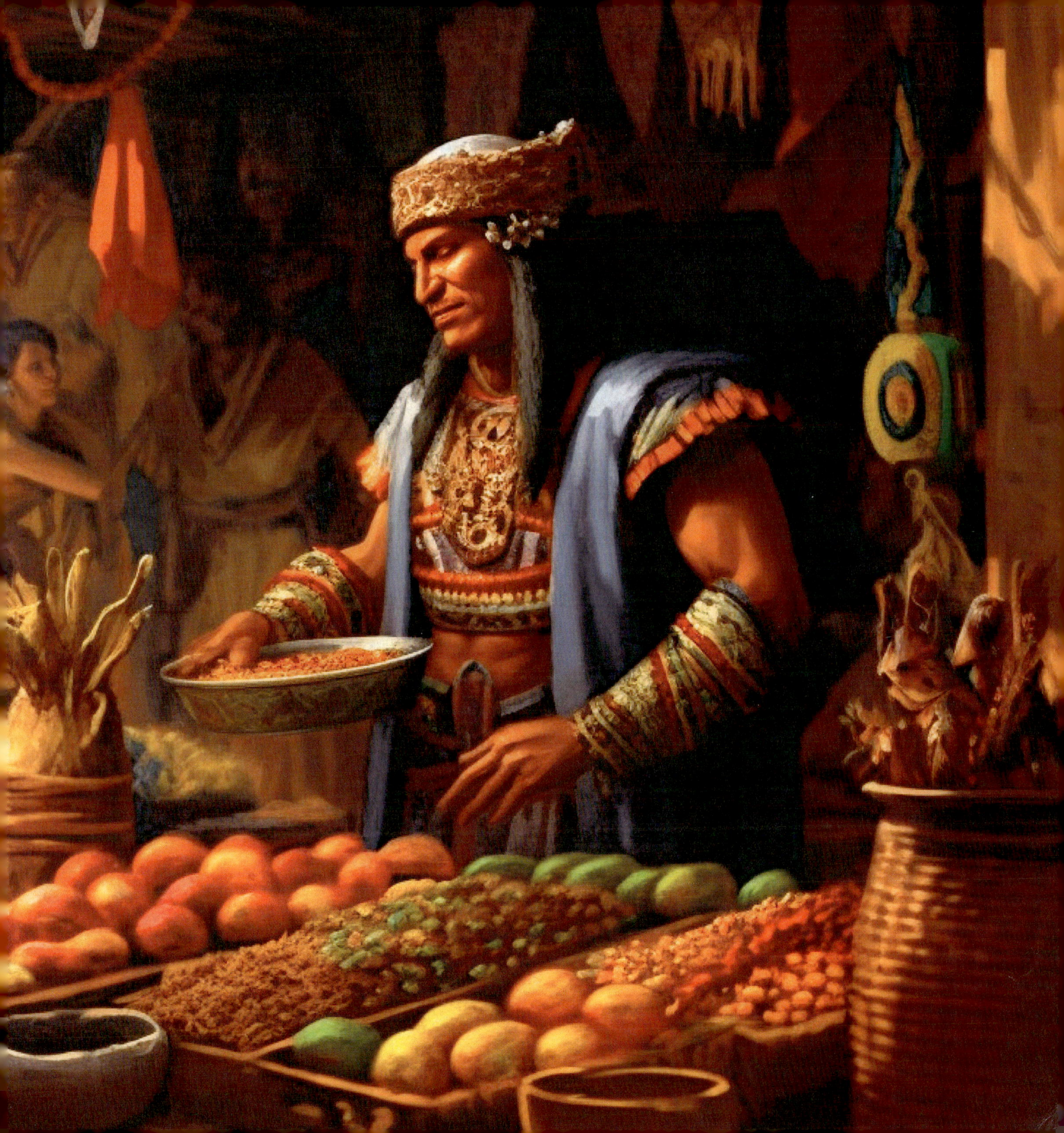

In the fields, the farmers sowed,
And with the sun's kiss, the crops they grow.
Maize and beans, and squash delight,
Under the sun's warm, nurturing light.

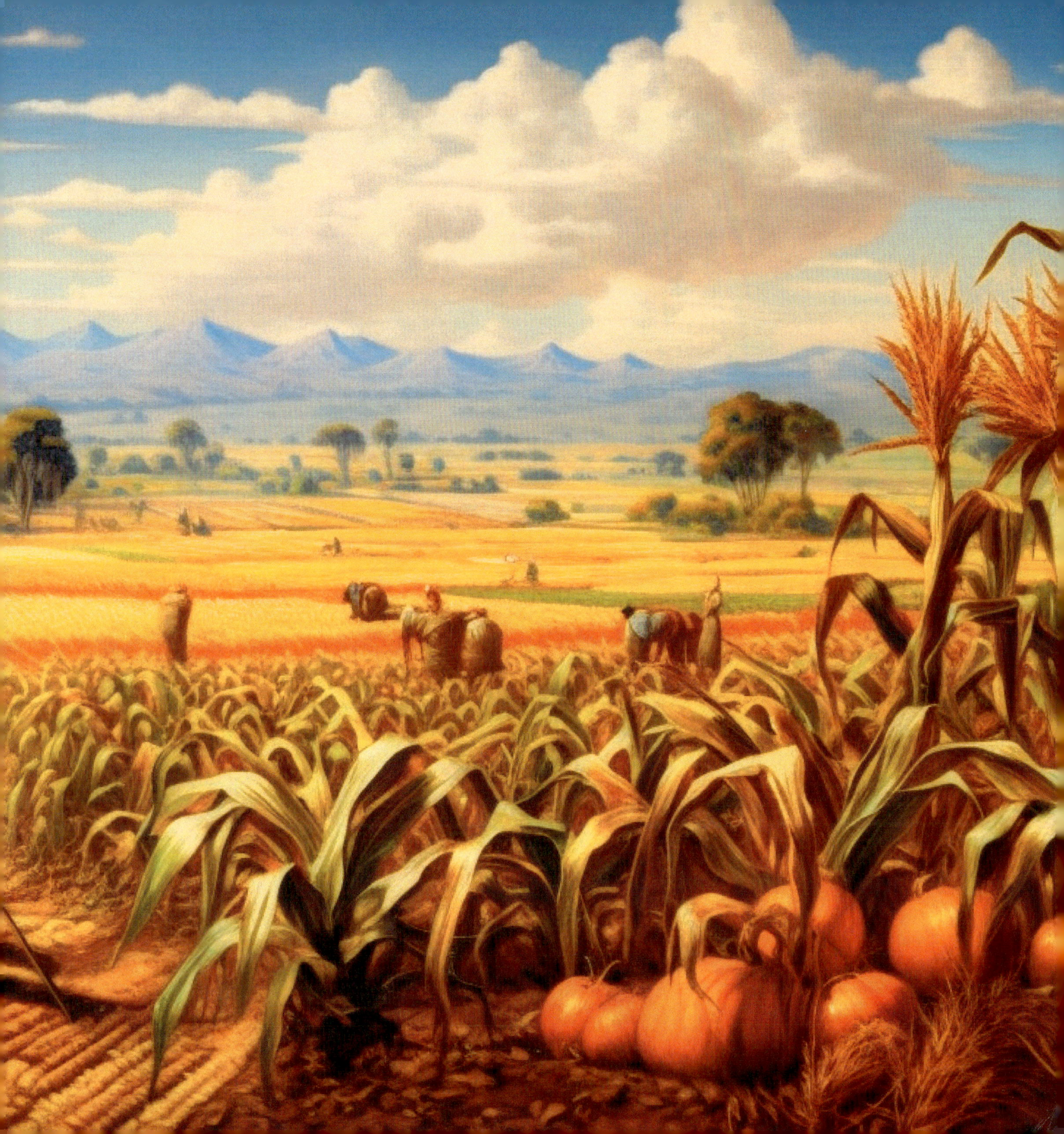

Aztecs had a pantheon, gods galore,
To whom they prayed, their spirits to restore.
Quetzalcoatl, the feathered serpent, a god so wise,
His tales are an adventure, full of surprise.

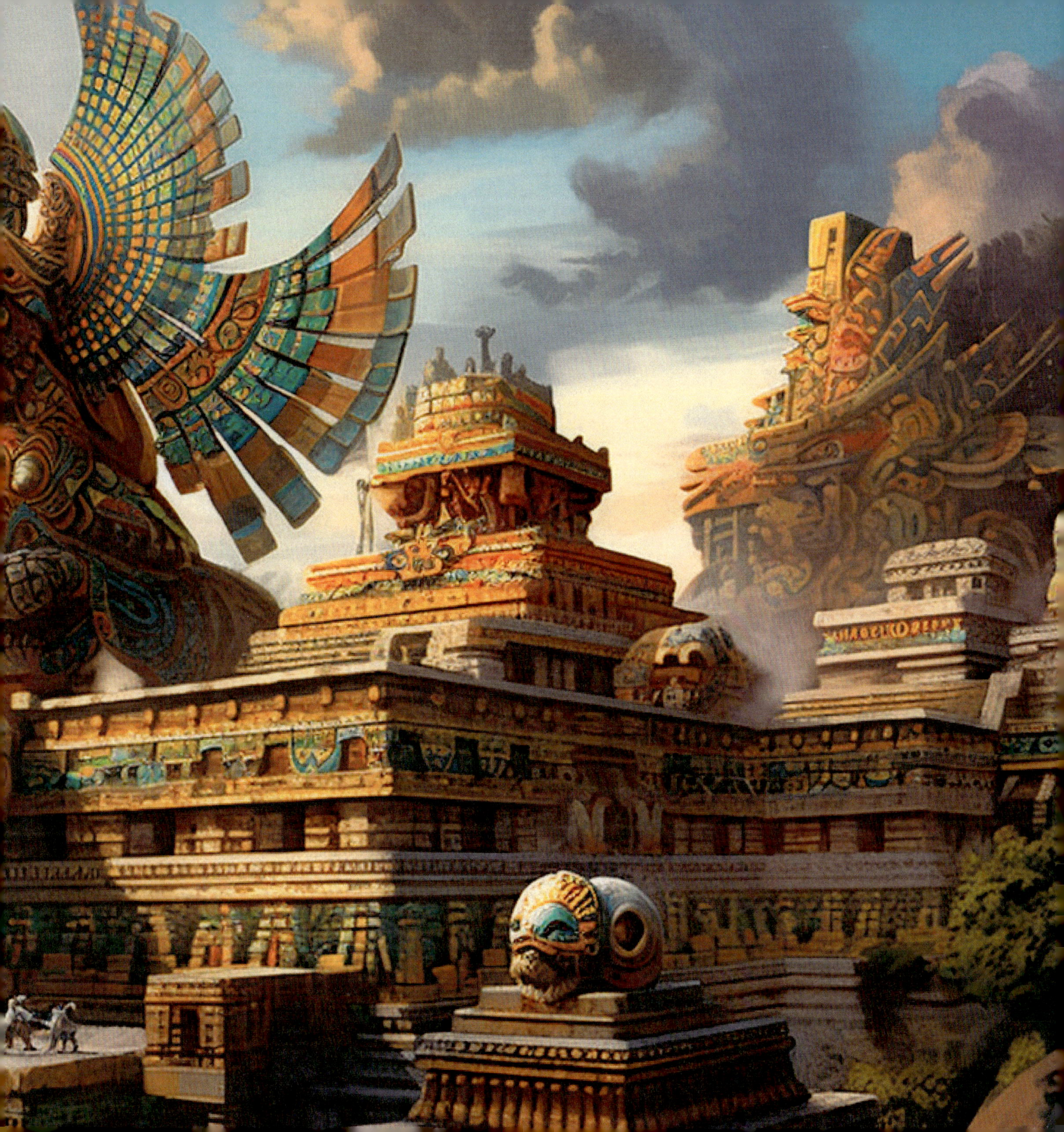

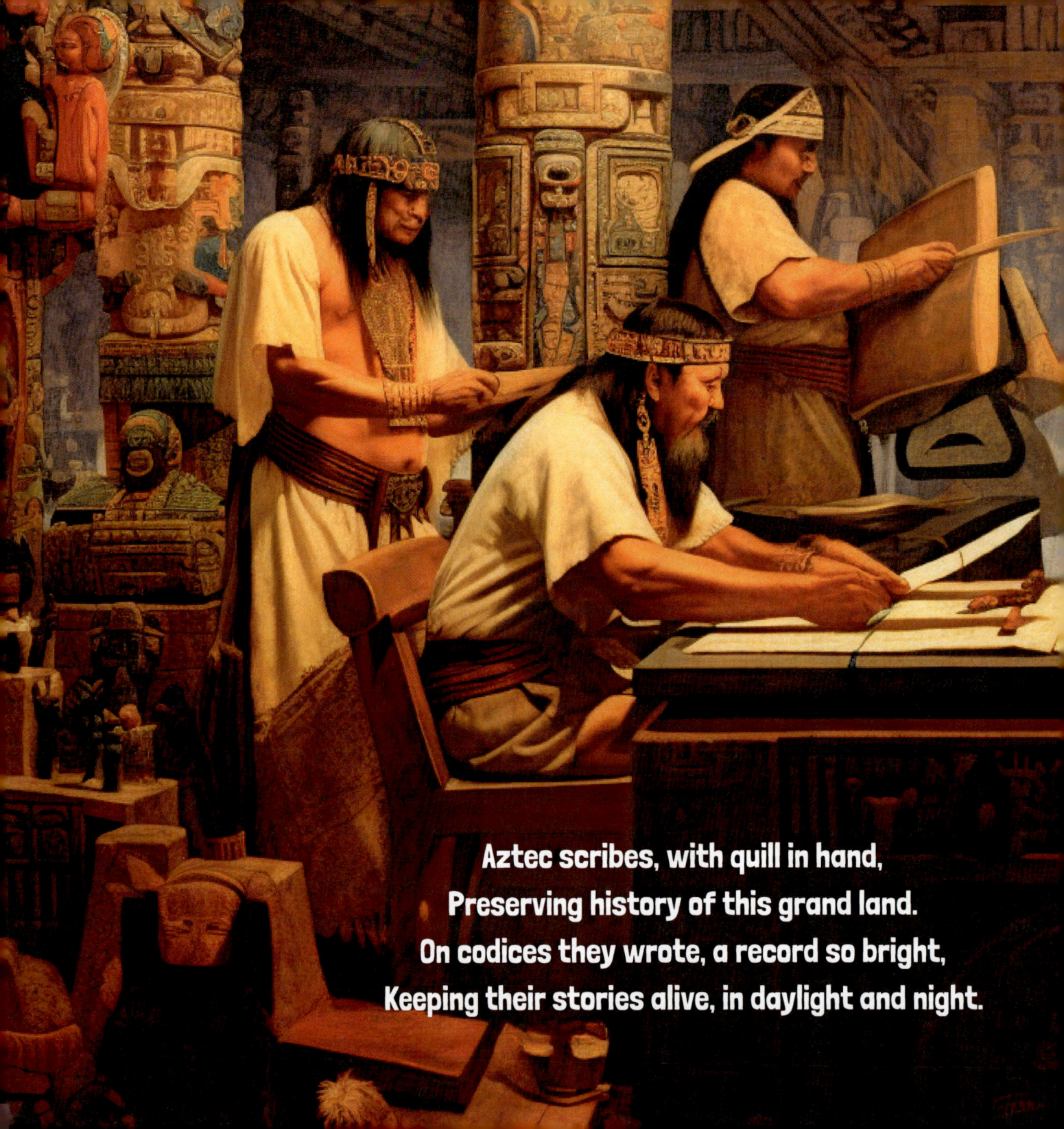

Aztec scribes, with quill in hand,
Preserving history of this grand land.
On codices they wrote, a record so bright,
Keeping their stories alive, in daylight and night.

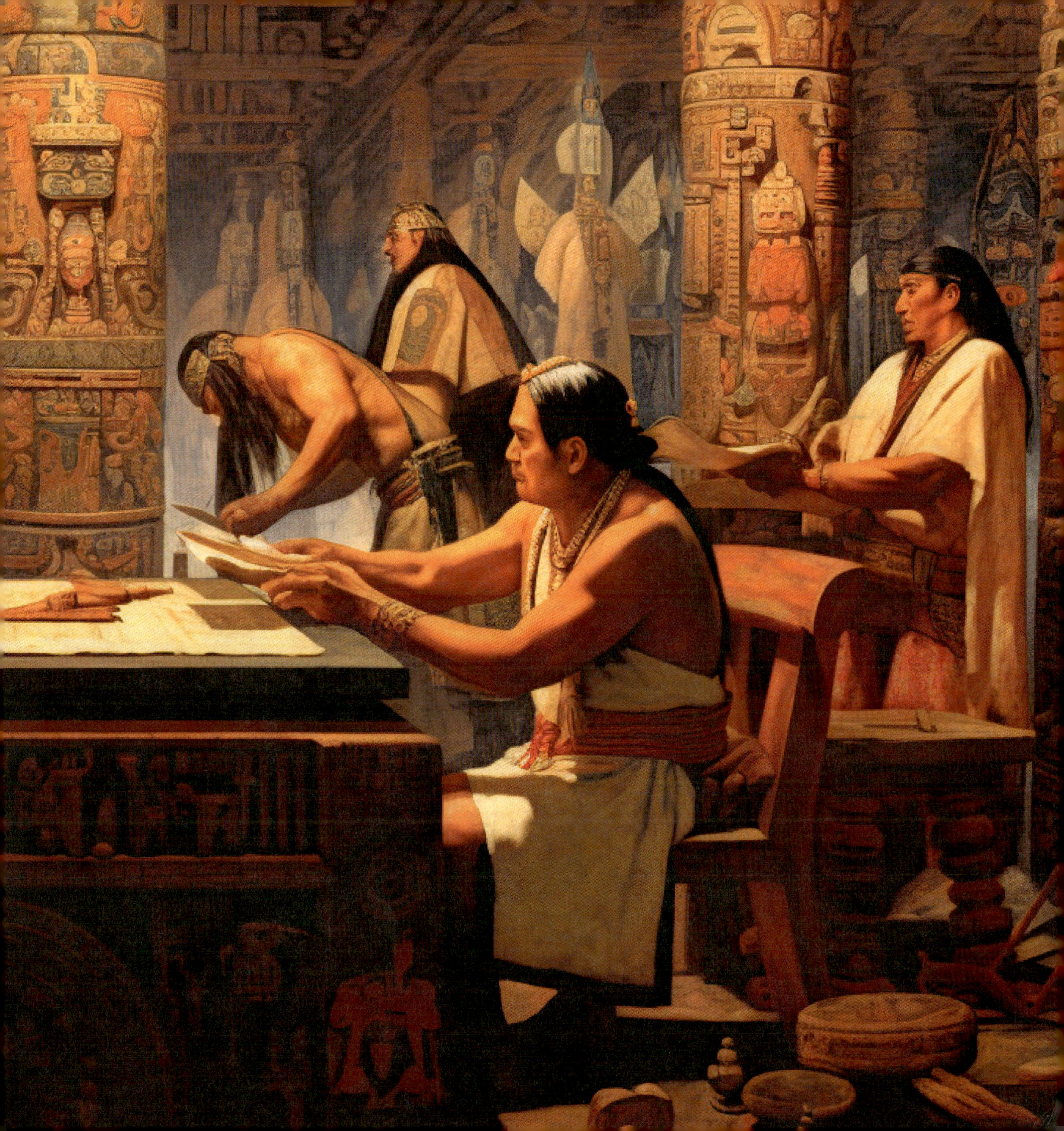

Delicious foods, they did cook and bake,
Tamales, tortillas, and even chocolate cake.
Corn was the hero, in every meal,
Their culinary prowess, it was real.

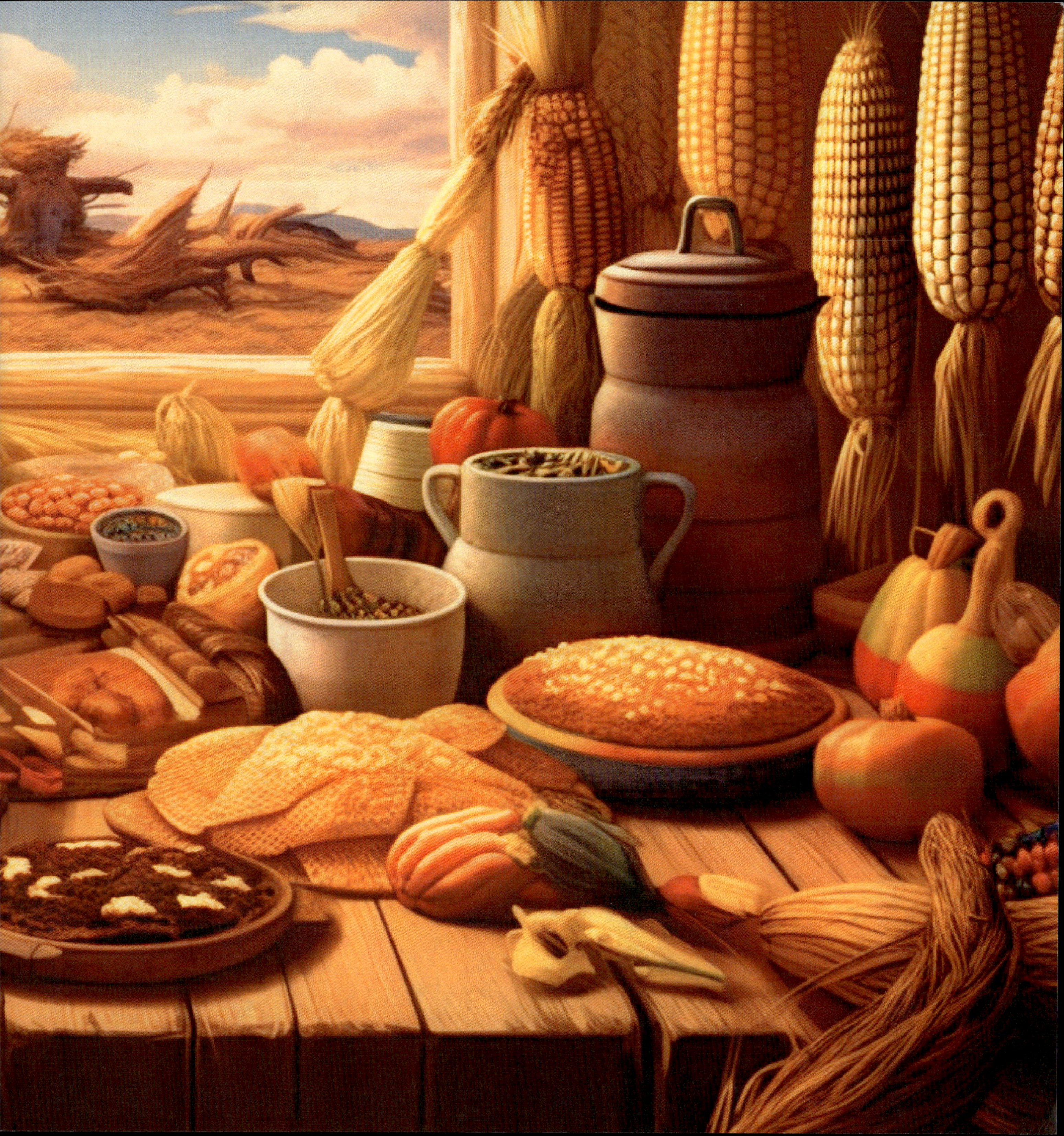

In Aztec lands, they dressed with flair,
Cotton tunics, and feather headdresses to wear.
Beads and feathers, colors so bright,
In the sun's warm glow, a delightful sight.

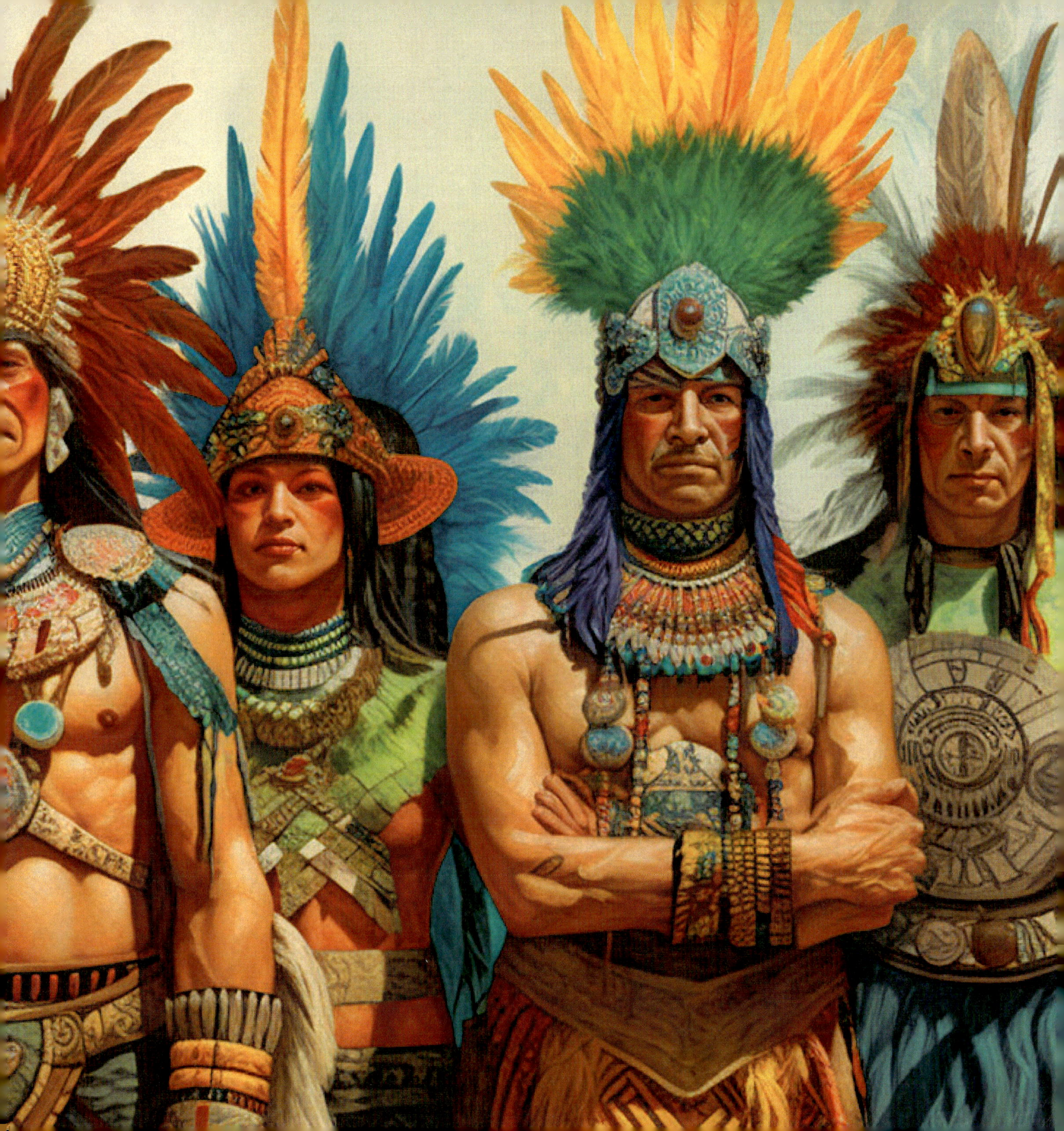

Aztec art, oh, what a sight,
In radiant hues, shown bold and bright.
Brightly painted pottery, and feather-work so fine,
Their artistic legacy, through time does shine.

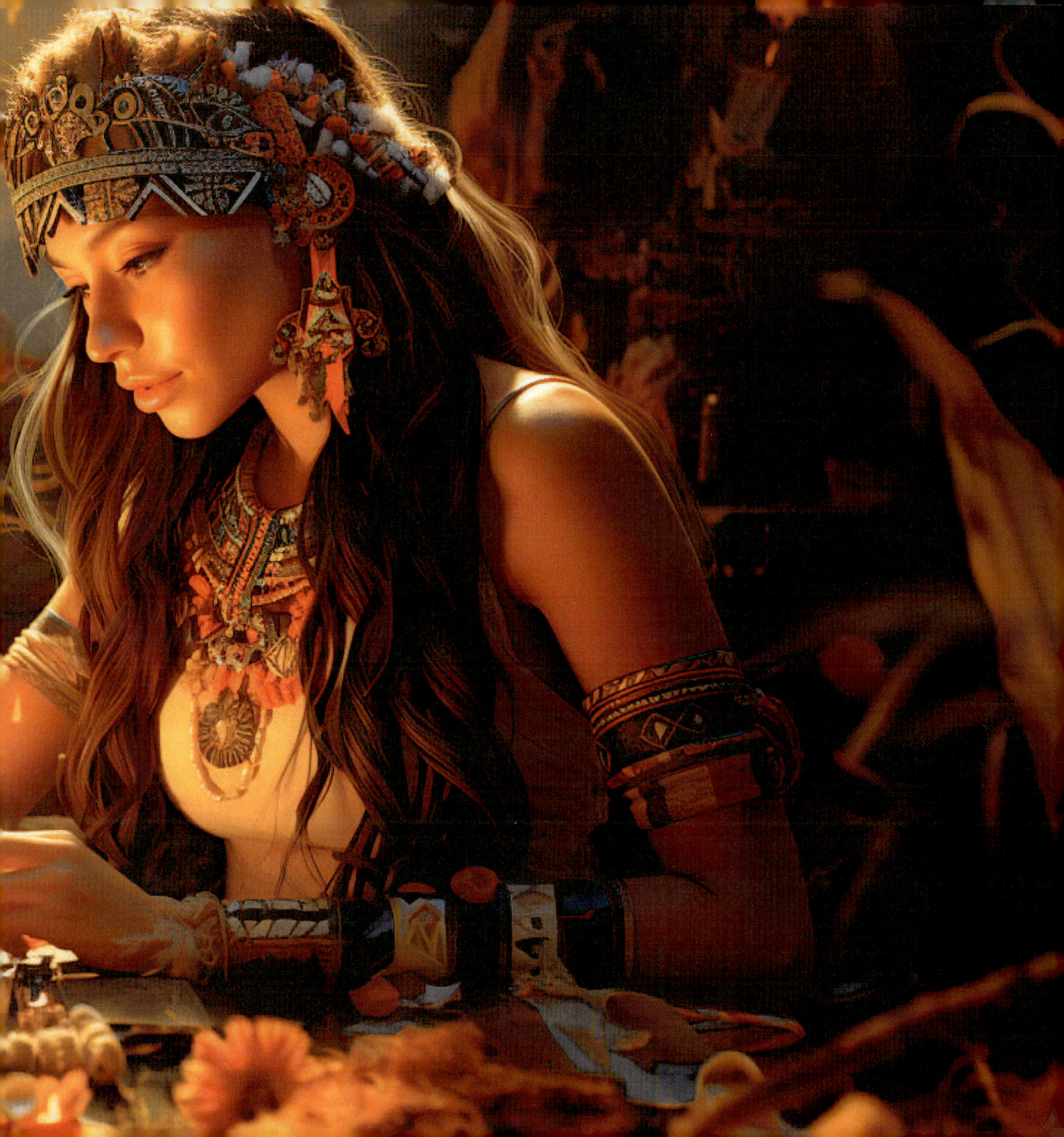

Science and learning, they held dear,
The heavens and stars, they'd watch and peer.
They'd map the skies and chart the land,
Their thirst for knowledge, forever grand.

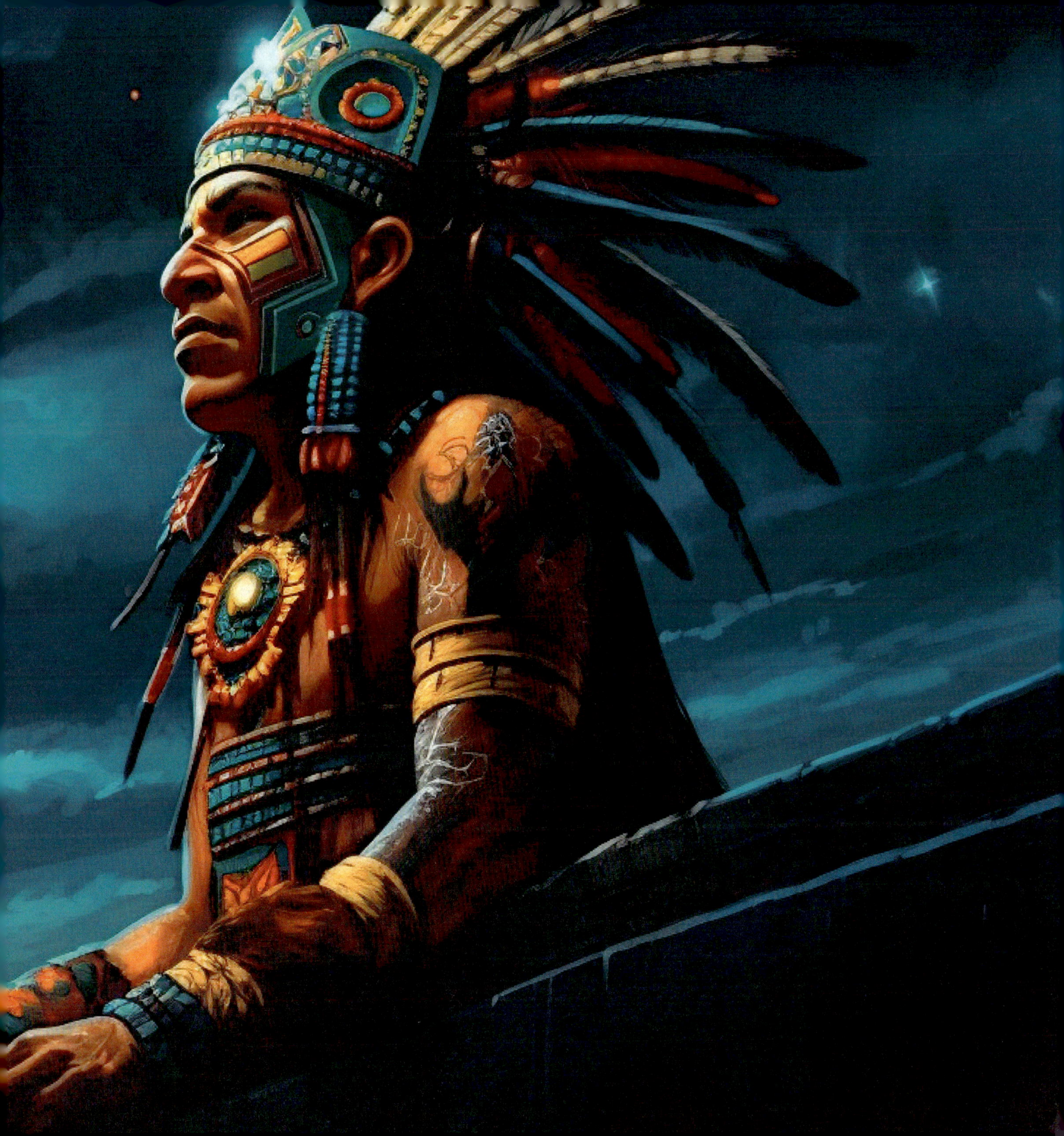

Religion was key, in Aztec life,
It guided them through peace and strife.
Temples high, and priests so wise,
To the heavens above, they cast their eyes.

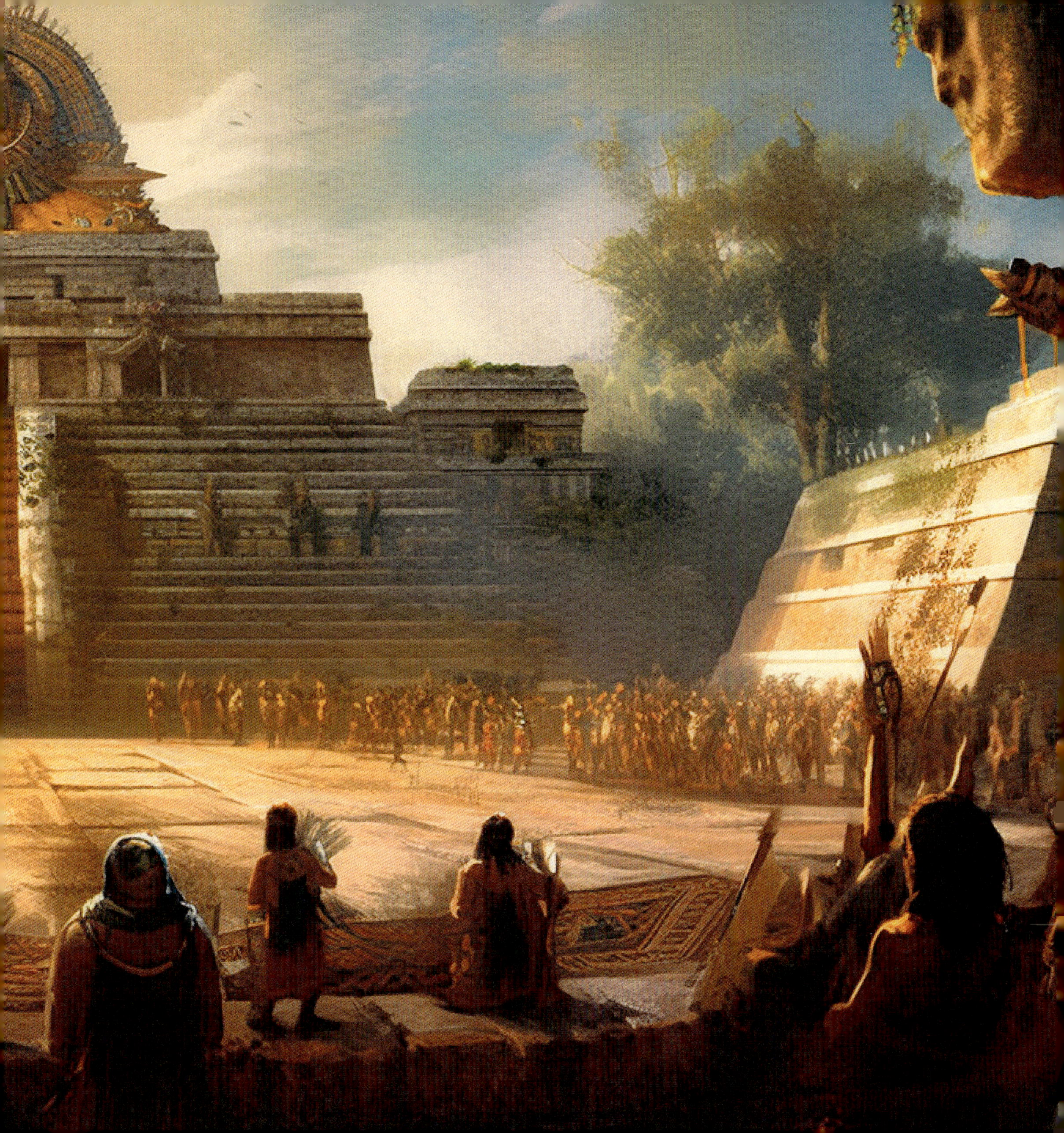

Music and dance, a joyful sound,
In every corner, it was found.
Drums and flutes, and voices raised,
In praise of the gods, they endlessly praised.

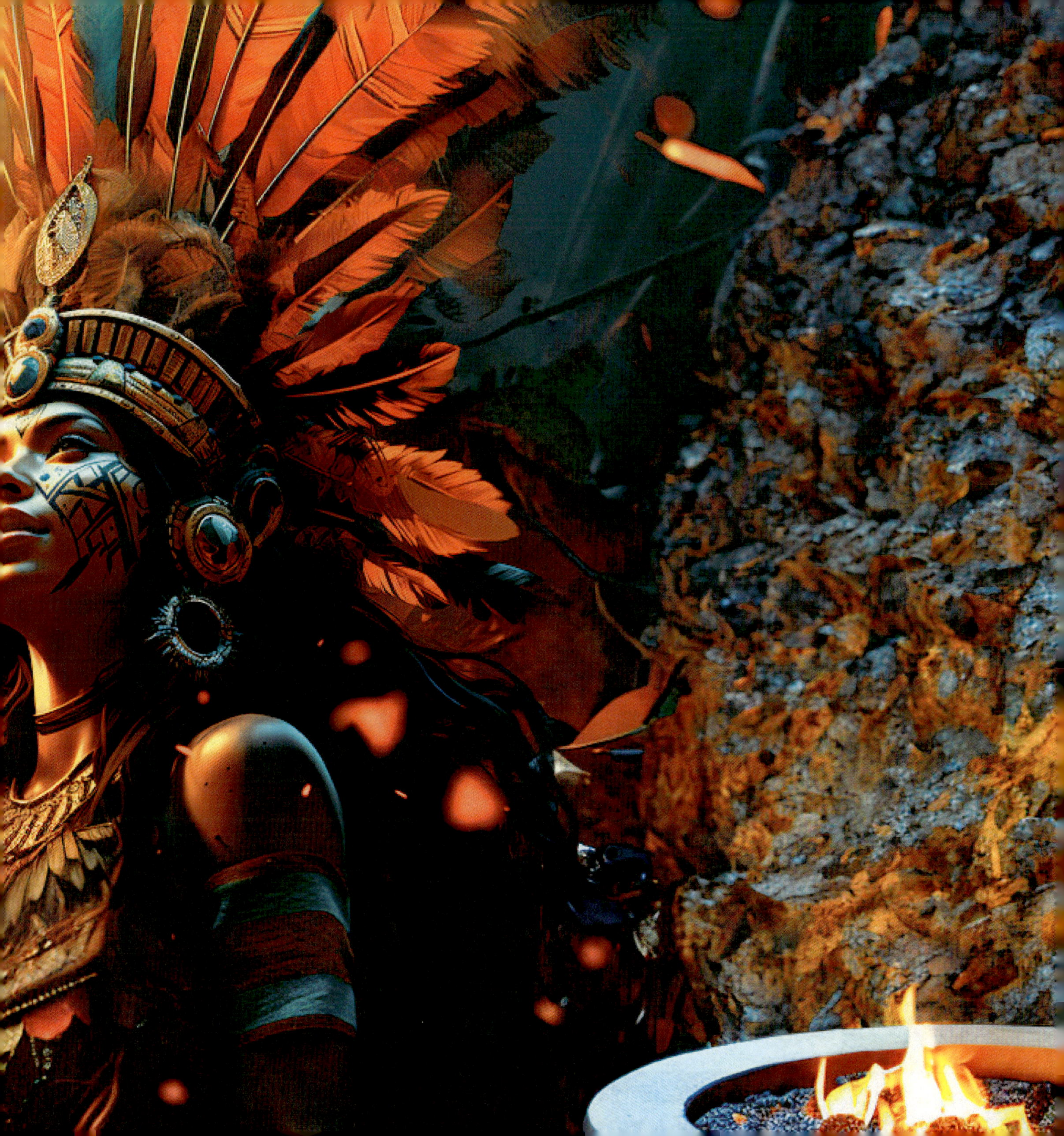

The Aztec people, with their hearts so bold,
In their community, both young and old,
With respect and honor, they lived each day,
In their unique, remarkable way.

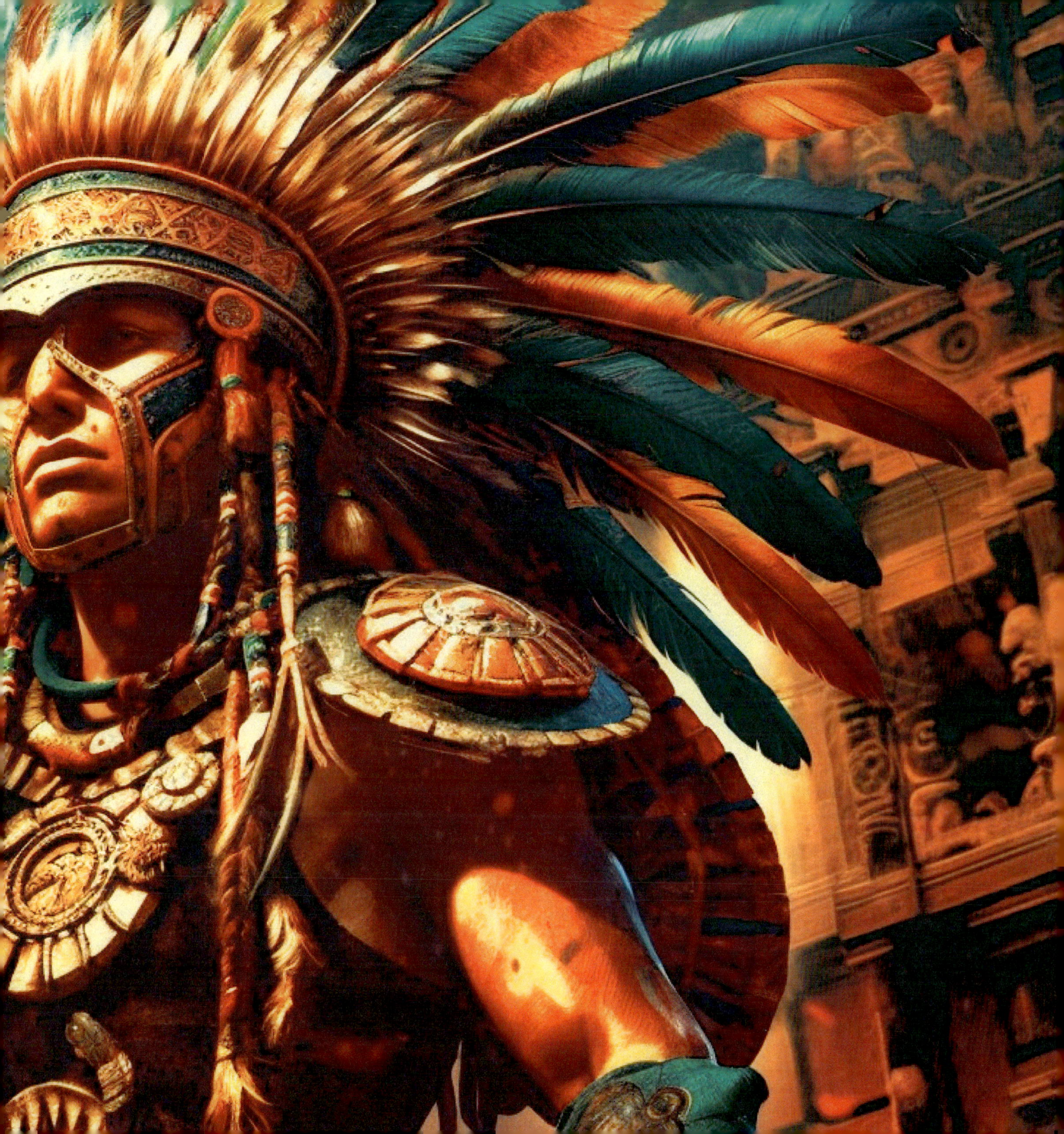

Through trials and triumphs, joy and sorrow,
The Aztec spirit, strong for tomorrow,
With a rich culture and history that's vast,
Their legacy is one that will forever last.

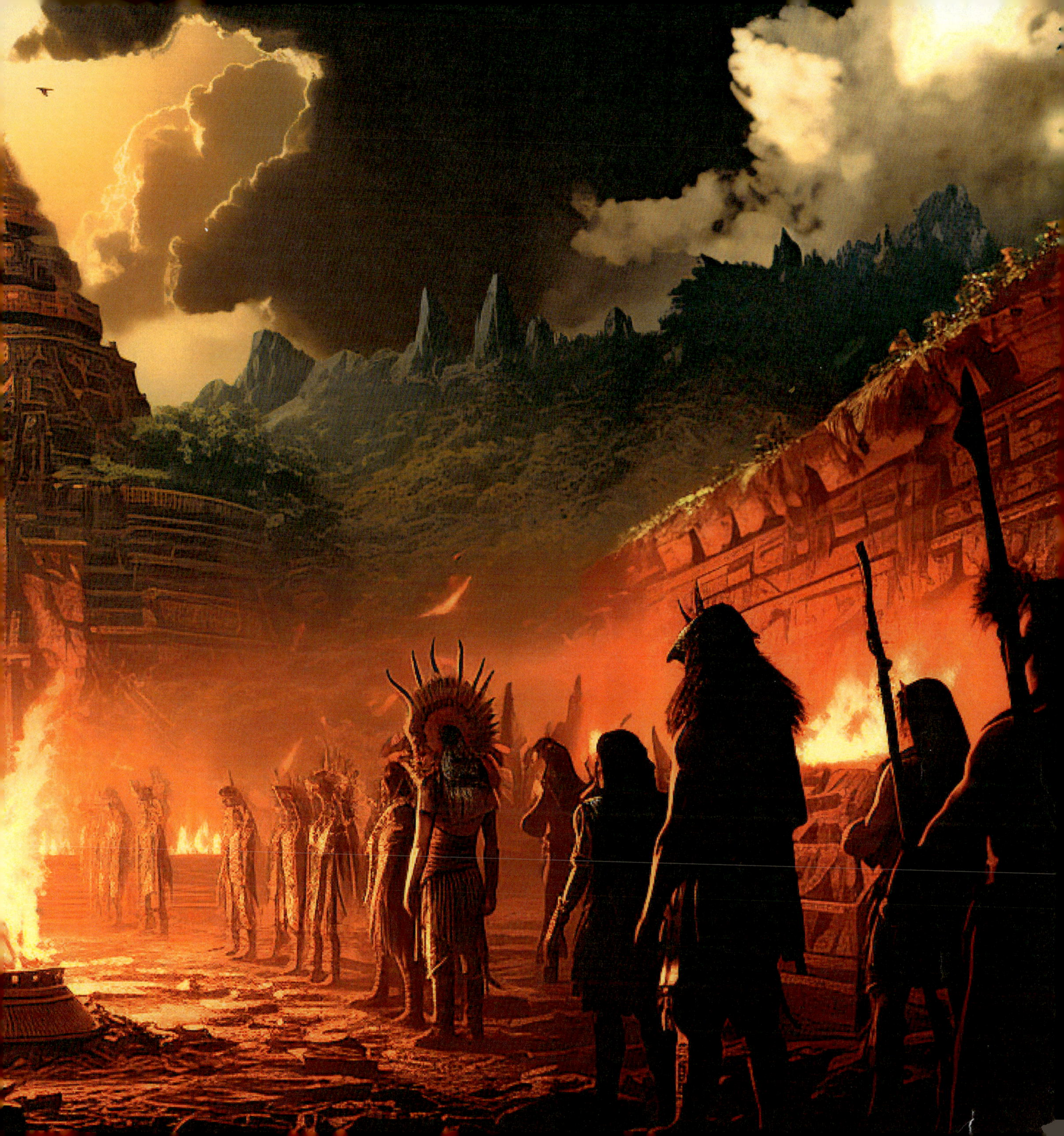

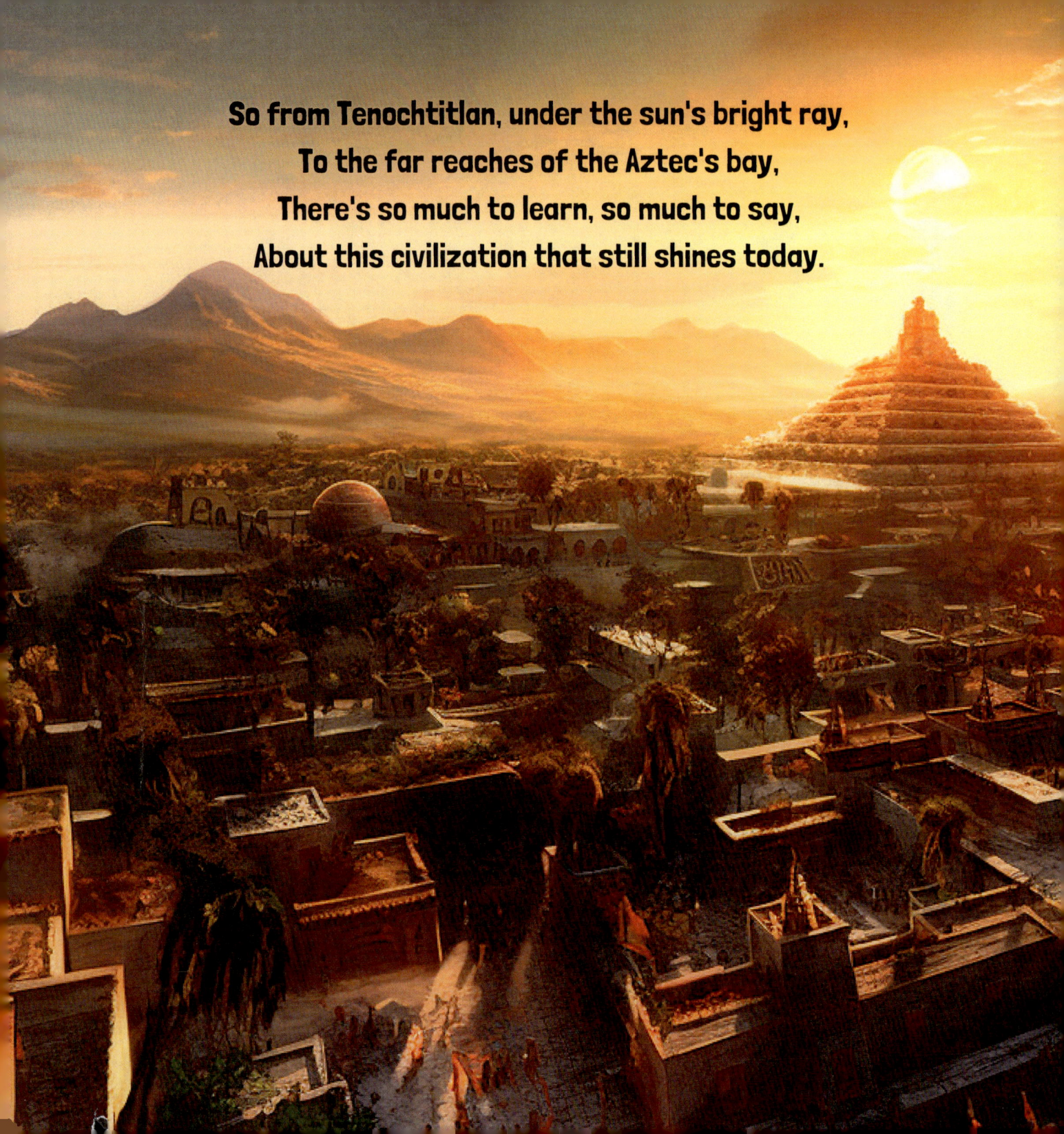

So from Tenochtitlan, under the sun's bright ray,
To the far reaches of the Aztec's bay,
There's so much to learn, so much to say,
About this civilization that still shines today.

And here we close our book of wonder,
Leaving us with so much to ponder.
The Aztec Empire, with its glory and might,
A civilization that still shines bright.

Made in United States
North Haven, CT
11 August 2024